I0545225

Conchas y Café Zine
Vol. III, Issue 3

Resonance
(resonancia)

a DSTL Arts publication

DSTL Arts presents

Resonance
(resonancia)

Conchas y Café Zine
Vol. III, Issue 3

Cover Design: Luis Antonio Pichardo

Book Design: Luis Antonio Pichardo

ISBN: 978-1-946081-15-5

10 9 8 7 6 5 4 3 2 1

www.DSTLArts.org

3529 Fletcher Dr.
Los Angeles, CA 90065

Table of Contents

starry night gaze
by John Khuu

Electric force field

Humming love songs, lusting long ago

Listen as her skin glistens 'neath starry skies

Eyes twinkle drowsily

    blink,

        smile,

            sleep

Beauty breathes in, breathes out

ESCRIBIR.
D. MANGAS

ESCRIBIR POR ESCRIBIR

ES SOLO CAMINAR

SIN SABER A DONDE IR.

LA CONCIENCIA DE ESCRIBIR

TE LLEVARA A EXISTIR

PARA REALMENTE VIVIR

ESCRIBIR ES DESCUBRIR

ES CONCEBIR, ES REVIVIR

ES RENACER Y ES UN MUCHO

MORIR....

LA VOZ ES LA ESPERANZA
QUE SE ESCUCHA
LA MENTIRA QUE DICTA
EL ETERNO CONFLICTO!!

JOSEFINA CAMINA
CONTRA EL VIENTO
Y LA ESPUMA

P.O.N. Alliteration

There's a problem with my petunias.
Partly due to pesticides in my pot.
I'm purposely problematic.
Probably because I'm punk.

I'm othered and ostracized—
Often over-dramatic.
I'm not outgoing or outstanding.
I overcome these obstacles.

Notwithstanding nonsense,
I never neglect the truth.
My words are negative and nasty;
Now, next time, and nevermore.

3

Jerry's Backyard Bird Adventure

To miscalculate the backyards fabricated grass would complicate

Jerry's treasure, a bird hunting adventure,

Into a risky venture

A noisy approach in this fragrant acre

Is an alert to his misbehavior?

Of being on the prowl for a tasty morsel

Hoping to see jubilee of game in the orange tree

Jerry hides in the leaves

Creeps through branches

For the feathered creatures

Seem unaware

"No, Jerry"

His beloved's voice, shouts

Catapults fowls to the sky

Chaotic kaleidoscope clamor

Jumping down, loving bumping against her

Porcelain skin beauty

Looks angrily at him, a grim grin

Feeling small, his lous blossom appall

Jerry heads for the wall

Sitting cattywampus not to fall

Screechy sparrows strike

Swiping grey paw, he fights

As his petite, bittersweet amore

Retreats inside

Quickly springing downward into rocky camouflage

The attack turns to another cat, Garlic

Nemesis, proxy

Creates a paradoxy, she runs away, no moxie

Queen of his heart returns

To the garden, with cat food, setting on his matt

Caressing pat for this Korat cat

She woos Jerry, her boo,

As he purrs,

That's what cats do

By Patsy Pantoja

The bad baby babbles backwards in a basket, at the backyard, with balloons and balls. A baber baking in the barn bacon, banana, and bat bagels. The bear hides behind a tree while eating beefy black beans.

Oscar O. Valencia

Untitled

Suzanne Im

ever since the crook
broke through
the black brick wall
–no joke
he cloaks himself in a hoax
that no one can coax
him out of
he smokes
with folks
and pokes
fun
at the oaks
for kicks
he'll fix kinks
in kitchen sinks
but
at night
he picks candle wicks
to light.

Goodnight my Knight

Goodnight my brave knight

Your might lights the night

Like white moon so bright

Quite a bite of delight

Wine scent of metal

Fine acts of chivalry

Glorious to me

Ideal nobleman

Cease, halt my breath

Soon hums in June tune

Endless interlude

Mood hewed my prude

Oh rude nude essence

Oh tenacious stare

Eyes a pair so rare

Hair fair, do I dare?

Not tonight kind fight

So goodnight my knight

----_N. Yvette Hdz._---

Consiencia amaneciendo de sangres cosmicas

Un Renacimiento

Colección dentro mi cuerpo

Reconocimiento ancestral

Raizes curando, raizes naciendo

Desde mis aguas internal hay aguas sagradas

Creando canales adentro de mi cuerpo

Puro Conocimiento

Unidad está creciendo adentro

Gracias universo y creador por estos momentos

♥ Mar I sol

Tamahagane

Creation furnace scorching red
tradition alters simple sand
Old-Master hands reshape round-steel

Abraham J.
2018

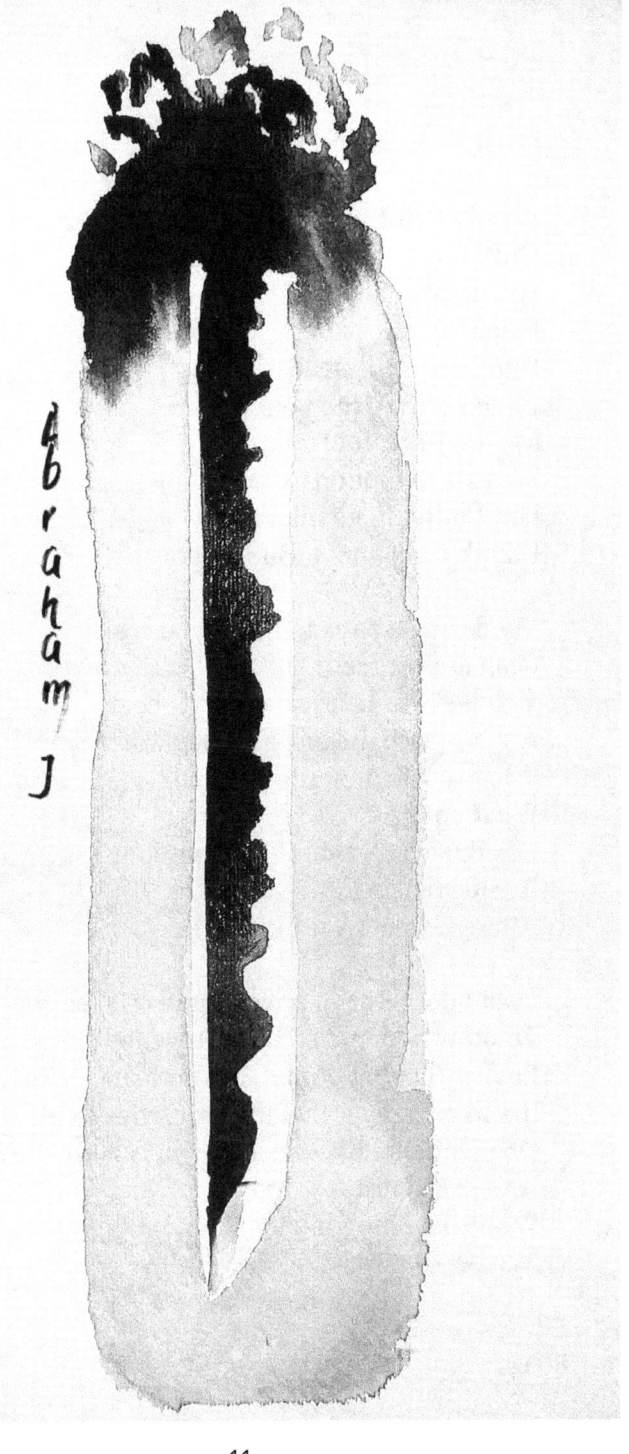

Abraham J

Desire   Karyn G.

I could build an empire or even higher
Out of feelings. These things
Are almost tangible,
Palpable, touchable.
But desire will never do.
It won't bring me you.
Maybe I'm a fool. What rule
Was set in motion, what potion
Did I drink to get like this.
I think I'm a mess. But I digress.

My desire aspires to make you real
I can almost feel
You here, so near, so close it seems
Are all these dreams a distraction?
What satisfaction for my soul?
What goal
Has the heart in this? It seems amiss,
A pathetic aim,
Almost lame. Am I insane?

Could desire have power, now or ever
To draw two, me and you, together?
I never thought of that, but perhaps
It's like a prayer that the air carries to
One who, not like me and you, can see the best
And put to rest my desire
With something higher
Maybe you, or who knows who.
That thought will have to do.

Blind Love
By Rocio Diaz

Imperfect human
beings, we are learning
as time ticks; pain builds
a wall preventing us
from what we really want
The us
There's love
unsaid,
it's there felt,
visibly expressed
invisibly seen,
invisibly said,
it's underneath
the pain, it's beneath our masks
distant as our souls could be,
and as close
as our inner children want to forgive.

It's between the words
we used to speak,
that is now, only air that beats,
but we are too stubborn
to admit, yes, indeed,
we still love
each other, a warmth
in the breath, a gentle
warmth that we hope
will still caress the love
that remains.

Enamorado

Este cuento será cantado por
un enamorado cabisbajo y disfrazado
de cometa sonrojado sin cuetes
disparado

Que el amanecer lo ha alcanzado
Beso no privado del romance ines-
perado.

— Fridey

Alma Gemela

Catalina, refugio
de mis sueños.
Catarata de agua cristalina.

Rostro cálido que me
enamora con su risa.
Voz que besa mis
oídos cada mañana.

Nombre romántico de
letras azucaradas.
Esposa mía, regalo de
Dios en esta vida.

Alma gemela que guía
mi barca cuando naufraga.
Mi mano escribe "te amo" y
nuestro corazón levanta el vuelo.

Raúl Macías Casas

Dick Loves Juicy
By Eddie Hall White, Jr.

Like an ice cube frying in a skillet, Juicy was a sensational, transformational chick
She smiled, flashed her goods and captured Dick, quick.

He loved her like a hog loved slop, liked hip loved hop.
Liked Rickey loved Lucy — that was how Dick loved Juicy.

Then

Eventually Juicy's dynamite curves grew wide.
But Dick loved Juicy inside.
All he saw was the nobility of her soul.

JUICY MADE DICK WHOLE.

16

Flowers for Stephanie

Out of all her former lovers, I'm the only one left
alive. Often, I find myself at her grave with flowers.
This candle still holds a flame.

Daily, my deepest desire; for decades she lived in
my dreams. Despite my advances, nothing became of us.
During daylight, hope becomes dust.

It's strange how sometimes solemnity gives way to sadness.
It's silly to reminisce on past events as I stand
alone with a bouquet of roses.

WORDS BY:
NIKOLAY
GARCIA

DRAWING
BY:
MERRY
FLOWERS

TRATARE!!.
D. MANGAS

TRATARE DE ENREDARTE

TRATARE DE ENREDARTE EN MIS PROMESAS
ROBARE EL EMBRUJO DE TUS OJOS
QUEBRARE LO SUTIL DE TU MIRADA.

TRATARE DE BEBER TU CUERPO ENTERO
QUE TU VOZ AHUYENTE
LA PRISION SILENCIOSA DE LA ALCOBA.

TRATARE DE TENERTE, DE ROPERTE
DE HACER DE TI EL ATAQUE FEROZ
DE UN LOBO HAMBRIENTO

TRATARE TRATARE
TRATARE AMADA MIA
DE ARRANCAR EL SEPULCRO
QUE DA EL TIEMPO....

Soñando del día cuando nuestros cuerpos estarán intimamente juntos

Movimientos del nacimiento tranquilo y profundo

Entregando besos al universo

Manos lentamente tocando tu piel de cacao sagrada

Bésame cariñosamente, en mi frente

Abriendo mi tercer ojo de intuición y compasión

Este sueño será una realidad con tu consentimiento

Camino paso por paso en la dirección del AMOR

♥ marisol

19

FUEGO

Ardo en llamas
por esas locas ganas
de cabalgar a tu lado
de quemarme en el pecado
por el fuego
por ese ardiente deseo
dulce amarga obsesión
de conquistar esa boca
y lograr esa fusión
que calcina, que provoca...
Ah..tu boca, tu corazón..
es todo lo que yo quiero
el luchar por ese anhelo
de lograr una amalgama
con tu esencia y con la mía
para alcanzar esa orilla
que me llama
llamarada que me quema y que me sana.

Ana C. Holton.

Just Take Your Shit

Mauricio Moreno

My place was here | You let me die
Your face was queer | I could not hide
The storm you quelled | I could not fight
You saved my head | But killed my light

Through all your words | You kept me high
Though af-ter you | I found no sky
Forc-ing my hand | You fright-ened me
Your sub-tle grip | It poise-ned me

The sweet em-brace | Your wick-ed kiss
The gent-le touch | It left a cyst
Your cod-dled words | They formed a mass
Tor-ment-ed days | These, too, shall pass
Or So they Say | Those lies were true
I could not kill | The mem'ry of you

You stripped my fears | and gave me sins
My che-mis-try | the code with-in
The D-NA | And ev-ery strand
was shat-tered with | the mas-ter plan

A cre-vice, there | is where you lie
Be-hind my eyes | is where you hide
Be-tween your legs | I conquered you
In-side my soul | You conquered me

Just take your shit | and leave me be
I try to kill | with a-pa-thy
I scream ag-ainst | a mut-ed wall
It screams and says | "you lost is all"

To-mo-rrow comes | I want you gone
No bit-ter tears | for los-ing pawns
You've won the game | and won the con
Just take your shit | and leave by dawn

What it Means to No

Suzanne Im

There is dissent over consent
Dainty flowers blown, plucked, and bent
Gates of grey open for a gent
Fingers prod, then point outwardly;
She repents for what came and went.

Burden borne silently no more
Scores have awoken to implore
Don't lay the blame on what she wore
Such arguments are cowardly
We'll overturn what came before.

No more sex in acquiescence
Nor in blatant nonacceptance
Let strength sweep over diffidence
Voices merged rise powerfully—
As truth brims in their eminence.

Down Whittier Boulevard

Poppin', rockin', jumpin', holla

On a low-rider 63' Impala

Down Whittier Boulevard

Homies best of cronies

Even the Po-po won't

Mess this groove,

Car clubs on the move

Mural hoods round the boulevard, Yo

Chilin', feelin' the vibe

Tightness of the tribe's ritual ride

Ain't nobody chingón

We're the jewel of East L.A., cool

Internet, hell our numbers swell

Rollin' we're bouncin' free

Everybody know me

Party jammin', how it's gonna be

Ridin' pura raza, pura vida

Mala yerba goes around

Oldies sounds, blast this town

No trippin', just keepin' it real

La familia cruisin' hard steel

On Whittier Boulevard....

By Patsy Pantoja

Procrastination

Michelle Smith

To be a day late,
and an hour behind,
means to yourself you are not very kind,
for procrastination is the devil in disguise,
because indeed to yourself,
you do lie.

Fabiola Manriquez

Marijuana

Marijuana is for Juana

And Madona

Y la Marrana

e.p.   karyn g.

elephant.

effortlessly elevated,
an eminent empire,
exquisite example
of evading extinction.
enormous eyes,
elegant ears.

imponderable pulchritude,
ponderous poundage.
a palpable presence, properly
providing plentiful portly pleasure,
pounding apace.
prominent, pliable proboscis.

pachyderm,
peacefully partaking of peanuts.

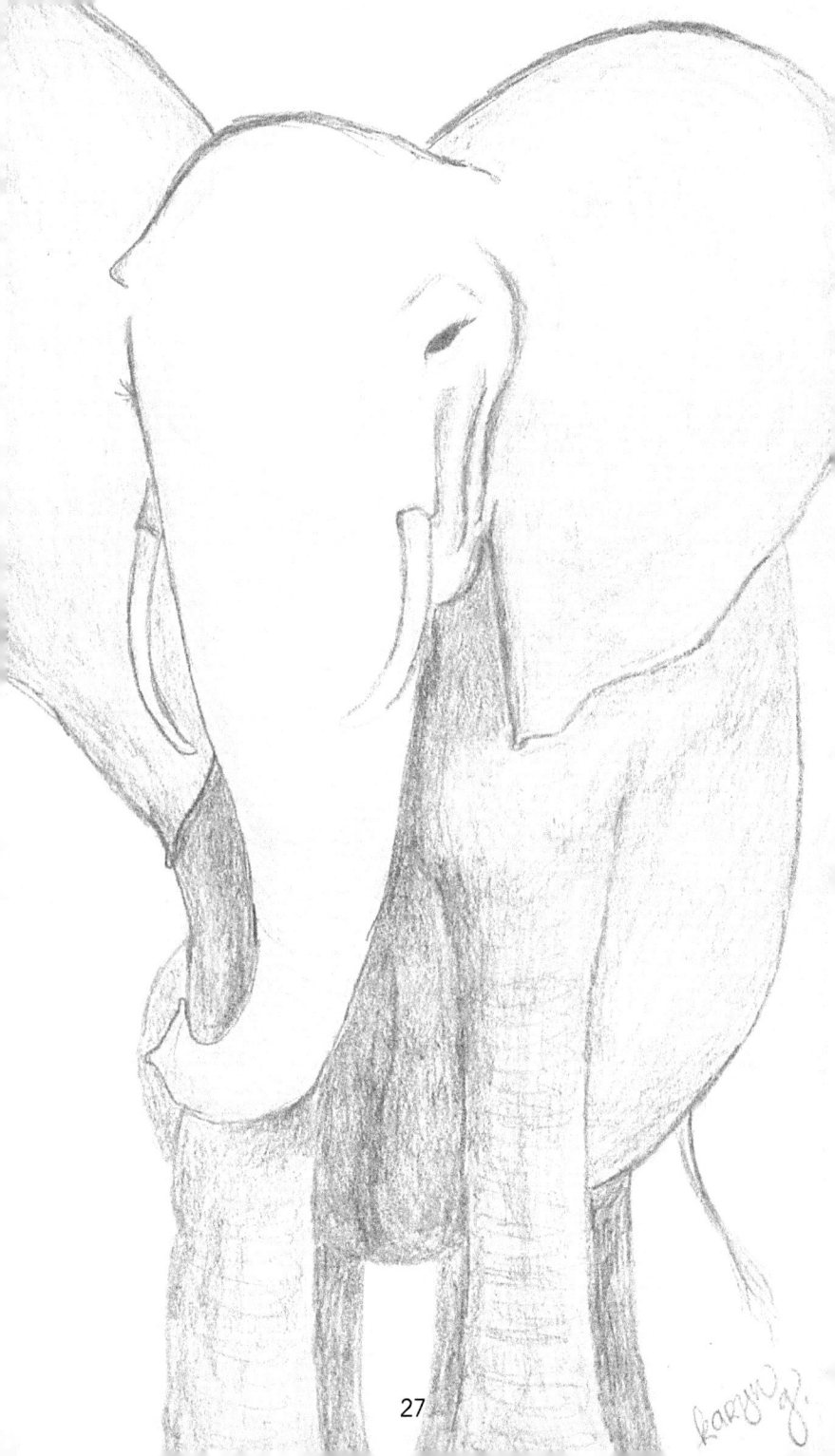

"CH"

Chillé como la chilindrina
El cheese se cayo
a la chingada.
I choose   the church
    to   chill at.
Chainsaws   of chocolaty
chambers   torture me
Oh! chariots   of charmers
eating   chalupas
    a   cucharada
while   childish

cheetahs chase a
    Xoloitzcuintli.
            Alicia M Rodriguez

28

<u>the old crow</u>
by David Fallon
the old crow
black as mold
folds its wings
he does not sing
instead he croaks
the anguished choke
of an angry bloke
with his beak
and a few fast tweaks
he strokes his worn
and weathered feathers clean
he hops into the heather
stopping to peck at leaves
flecking aside the bark
of rotting trees
he spots an occasional louse
and the corpse of a small mouse
covered in juicy house flies
being a spry bird
he looks up at the sky
and wonders why
why he walks upon the land
why he drifts above the sand
why he is hunted by man
why he has no hands
with hands
he would break the man's back
tear him open
like a paper sack
but it is not meant to be
so he watches
and when man appears
he flees
and prays to see the day
when the way of man fades away

The little turtle and
beetle battle for a
skittle, because of this
they startle and rattle
the cattle, who
trample and crumble
purple people eating
an apple.

Oscar O. Palencia

Baking Apples In My Loud Home

Smelling Baked Goods With My Long Nose

Big Ears Hearing The Breeze In Trees

Love My Friends Whom Eat My Treats

By
Ziba
Zehdar-Gazdecki

Tamal de Piña color de un tucán

Colores amarillos brillando y los verdes
mezmorisando los bosques de su tierra natal

Sabor sensacional de maíz tierno

Dejando la lengua y tu saliva bien dulce

Tamal de piña color de un tucan

Estas reanimando las memorias ancestral

Con cada modida escucho tu voz

Mensajes dulces y llenos de dios

VmarIsoL

Frida

Tengo una gatita
que es muy traviecita
que siempre
juega a la cacita.
que linda gatita
que gatita
tan traviecita,
que come y brinca
en su cacita,
que gatita
tan preciosita ,
que pensará
la gatita siempre
jugar en su cacita,
que linda gatita.

Ana Elizabeth Tovar

The Rising by Tina Fallon

The sun rises today
I see colors run by
Fiery egg yolks jammed together
Mornin' is bursting,
This days' begun!

Virtuous Virgins

Virtuous virgins
frequently vanish
in the boyish
smile of late —

Susan Chavez

Niña De Trapo

Pobre niña con cuerpo de trapo.
Quisiste correr, volar,
elevarte
al cielo.
Que clase de juego
te da la vida?
Porque tan cruel
se porta contigo?
Si llegaste como todos los niños,
orgullosa,feliz con tus manitas
abiertas al cielo,
No llores niña de trapo
sonriele a la vida
Que no te vea triste
con tu cuerpo de trapo.

Ana Elizabeth Tovar, G.

No me quieres sola..
Tristeza Por que tan serca de
mi? Por que tan Compañera? Me
eres tan Fiel que me da miedo.

Pero se que cuando el sol este
aqui tu, te iras y yo estare sin
sin ti, aunque no me quieras
Sola.

— Judy

Caballito blanco

¿Tienes algo para mi?

Claro que si, en esta canción

Es una invitación para olvidar,

Y cantar en la soledad

Canciones sobre los dolores

Vivo en un mundo profundo

Canto para salir de mi miseria

Reir para sentir el mundo

Bien, nos vamos entre

los ramos,

ni hablemos.

—Christian Valles

My Vicious Vision

Mauricio Moreno

Take the time
To chime in on the presence
of pen & ink in my mind,

Take the time
to feel sublime.

Subliminal, sudden shocks of static truth in a staccato of stunted
still beats that creep deep in the crevices of my fleece.

Fleeting fits of final verses and vivid curses perched inside
velvet purses.

Did you find your purpose? Was it beyond the surface?

Did you attract the fractured pact between your soul and take it back?

Or was the attack too hacked?
Was it my support that you lacked?
Did it make you go black?

Did you choose to lose just to prove that you were the fool?
Did you remember the way, guey? The way we started when we
were both astray?!

Did you know that I stayed?

As long as I could...

But stay complacent, I will no longer!
I will no longer sway from the path that we laid.
Not for you
Not for us.
This is my way
to say
Thank you.

So, please excuse my right choice to blaze past the face at my
own pace.
Fuck the chase!

I'm in my own race
Set my own stakes.

While you wither away on wayward waters of worry wrought with wretched wisps of of want and wishes, I'll set fire to my skin and let this vicious vision viscerate my inhibitions and scorch my doubts with such precision that from the ashes, is born my mission.

And this is mine, not your decision.

El tren de la vida

Lloraba la rama del árbol caído
la rana cantaba muy cerca del río
pasaba la vida de poco a poco, tranquila
el hombre pasaba siempre a mediodía.
Pensaba la anciana en el tiempo ido
en tantos otoños que dejo el olvido.
El tren pasa lento
siempre por la vía
saludan alegren niños de la villa.
Se mueren los sueños
Duermen los deseos
Pesan, pasan, pisan los años perdidos.
a donde se entierran amores fallidos
La luna se esconde
brillan las estrellas
siempre por las noches pasan cosas bellas
y llega la aurora
nace la mañana, llega el sol,
se asoma saludando al día suena la campana,
el tren de la villa
se va contoneando, viva la Alegría

Ana Holton
Poemas
Feb 24, 2018

Minority Money

Fabiola Manriquez

When you know
The numbers control
The flow of the dough
Then, you know
You have power

Where Are You From?

Suzanne Im

> I may be silent, but I'm thinking.
> I may not talk, but don't mistake me for a wall.
> – Shigeji Tsuboi

With surprise upon our introduction
You tell me that my English is perfect
That there is no trace of any accent
Assuming that I must be foreign-born
This Californian transplanted in corn

Such moments deny manifestation
Summons presence to its destination

Yet prejudice exists in brilliance
A colleague who knows I am immigrant
Progeny offers this advice to me:
"To win, speak more like an American.
In other words, the opposite of you."
I brood over what this means as I move
Through conversations that breed doubt anew

Borders become barriers to entry
Make me feel like my mind is a prison
Yes, even though my mind is a prism
Hence I develop John Henryism
Broca's area is my enemy
Like parrots I fall back on mimicry

It's a delicate dance with two left feet
I enter the nexus where parties meet
Anxious not to sound banal or blasé
I impart less than perfect repartee

Often beach ball launch'd turns into beached whale
And bystanders turn to scope out the wave

Small talk weighed with Morse made context-heavy

Won't be when we're buoyant with empathy
Hear me out, offer generosity
Tensile strength can only get us so far
Mincing words spawns relations subpar

Let's meet at the fence and talk for a while
Approach offenses with a balanced eye
Familiarity fortifies sense
Weather can distract from impermanence
Come sit and commune without the pretense
Together, in comfortable silence.

Chapines en Chapinlandia

Ana C. Holton

Nacho Chavez, Chema Chicas,
Chico el chenco y Chon el cholo
choferes de profesión
chupaban en su changarro.
Dos chontes, chumos, chismosos
desde una choza, choteaban.
Chalo, el chonte más chavalo
dijo a Chente el más chaparro
Los cacho y los cachimbiamos?
O les "damos chicharrón"?
Chinguémolos un poquito–
dijo el otro, el chavalito.
mas los otros escucharon
la chusma conversación,
y al llegar los invitaron
a una chupa, a la chicha
y a una chela,
que se les subió a la chola
y a pichinga los pusieron.
Y en la champa, en el changarro
Nacho, Chema, Chico, Chon,
Chente y Chalo
los chontes y los choferes,
como coches, chanchos, chuchos
chupando se la pasaron.

Happiness lies in the little moments,

Drinking wine with old friends,

Making love till night ends,

Seen your son as a grown man despite that in your eyes

he would always be your boy

Under its slopes we counted our blessings,

Without knowing the final countdown had already began —

Perhaps our hands, always ready with a whip to inflict pain,

Those poor souls in chains,

Our eternal stain,

Or perhaps, our corruption or our vanity are to blame,

Collapse —

All hope,

Eruption —

Disguised, The Mountain,

Brings flame and Death..!

Smoke and ash had frozen us in time,

But here, is no crime,

For this last moments may look dire,

They are our last, but not all —

Happiness lies in the little moments.

Title: Pompeii

Abraham J.
2018

Vida

Que loca la vida,
siempre juega
a las
adivinanzas,
adivina
que va a pasar,
dice la vida,
la vida siempre
tan loca
que me
quiere engañar,
al juego de las adivinanzas
que nunca
me déjà ganar,
la vida siempre
quiere ganar
el juego
donde ella adivina
que es lo
que va a pasar

Ana Elizabeth Tovar G

Ritmo

Abandon the Action of
  Addiction
Muzzled Puzzle of
Juggling Kumquats.
El Quetzal
se quedo quejando
Mientras bailo y bato
  Chocolate
al ritmo de bachata.

Alicia M. Rodriguez

The Bull That Fell In Love With the Moon

Mauricio Moreno

I once heard of a bull
His colors were dull
His horns had been blunted
and his legs were now stunted

But when the moon was her brightest
His heart was then lightest
When her face was full
So, Too, was the bull's.

He chased her at night.
He pranced, and took flight.
Dying with might
To be her first sight.

But when the sun showed his face
and started his race,
The moon left her place,
leaving only a space.

And during this space,
The bull showed no grace
to show his distaste
of the Moon's fleeting pace.

The day crept with yellow
and peace filled the meadow.
But the bull forced a bellow,
Which he sang A cappello.

One night, then another
The bull sought his lover.
No type of cover
Could mask the Bull's shudders.

Days of loud mourning

Filled the Bull's yearning

Until the gods showed compassion
and released the Bull's passion

Full of fury and fire,
though weary and tired
He screamed his desire
Until his proud body retired

The gods heard his plea
and acknowledged his love
They granted him solace
In the heavens above

When he opened his eyes
To his wondrous surprise
The Moon shined before him
and revealed her disguise

"Now, we're together,
My Beautiful Light."
"In the darkest of nights,
you're my eternal sight."

So goes the legend
of Taurus the Bull
The story of the Bull
That fell in love with the moon

Breathless No More

I tried to let life run
    without regrets and misery.
Every day I had a chance
    to be someone I could understand.
Every night I thought of you
    and the world was nowhere in view.
I hoped, prayed and dreamed
    but you were not there.
I cried, prayed and sat
    and I found my breath.

by Claudia Mera Lam

52

Mi Amor
By Rocio Diaz

Se te extraña
Cada mañana
Porque este sentimiento nunca me engaña
Se me cuelga en el alma
Como una telaraña
Porque si es cierto
Todavía te amo
Té quiero
Te extraño
Pero con un gran dolor
Pronto tendré que arrancarte de mi alma
Y decirte hasta mañana

Un sueño

Cada noche voy al cielo
voy a buscar a mi madre
ella me espera sonriente
le hablo, regresa, ruego,
Madre regresa, despierta,
Tu sueño no es bueno
Que no ves como sufro
Estoy desvanecida
Tengo tiempo sola
Te estoy esperando
No solo una sonrisa
Despierta conmigo
Madre, madre bendita.

Ana Elizabeth Tovar G.

" OLAS "

D. MANGAS.
(FRANCES. COMPAÑERA DE VIENTO.
PRONTO LLEGAREMOS.
LAS GAVIOTAS ANUNCIAN)

REVERBEREANTES
GAVIOTAS FANTASMAS
BRUÑIDAS DE TIEMPO

OLAS QUE PERSIGUEN
REFLEJOS DE SOMBRAS

ETERNO VAIVEN
QUE SE TORNA CANTO
A LA ETERNIDAD

HACIA DONDE VAGAN
MANOJOS DE BRISA.
CUAL ES SU DESTINO
ARRULLOS BOREALES?

BUSCAN LA MIRADA
DE UN TRISTE PIRATA
O SOLO SON ALMAS
BUSCANDO DESCANSO
EN LA ETERNIDAD?.....

Sweet Potato Soul

Michelle Smith

Reminds me of back home,
Where the buffalo don't roam,
Not where the antelope don't play.
Instead,
I'm baking a pie
In a deluxe apartment in the sky
And there is a glow,
That when tomorrow unfolds
Another story
Which blooms like Morning Glory
I am not a spring chicken,
I'm a wise hen,
Gentrification will not make me Break or bend.
I hunger for for peace,
And desire to complete
So in my neighborhood and residence,
There's no need to compete.
My Sweet Potato Soul has weaponry,
Black and Brown especially.

El sabor del Son

Mire! compadre Simón
ya llegaron con su Son
los del pueblo de Atolón.

Vamos a ver si el patrón
nos da su autorización
para que empiece el danzón.

Se oye la voz del Señor
gritando a todo pulmón
que comience la función.

Aquí en esta hermosa región
el Son es una expresión
arraigada en la tradición.

Es un ritmo que se canta
con la voz del corazón
que la gente lo baila
con alegría y pasión.

Es una gran emoción
escuchar tocar un Son
porque sientes en los pies
cosquilleo y picazón.

Es una grata experiencia
poder zapatear un Son
pues el cuerpo se libera
hasta de la alta presión.

Te mostrare compañero
como bailo este Son
pues con seis vasos de ron
seguro pierdo la razón.

Bailar con gusto y talón
el rico ritmo del Son
te baja el colesterol
y te quita la tensión.

No me quiero despedir
sin antes a bien decir
que el Son es medicinal.
Lo debe usted saborear
Al momento de bailar.

Raúl Macías Casas.

Sunday Skating Syncopation

by John Khuu

Skateboarders' boards chop up the Sunday park sounds

Wheels clack between the sidewalk cracks

Spin-spin, clack-clack, spin-spin, clack-clack...

Whoosh –

Hear that ollie?

Two Minutes to Midnight

Two minutes to midnight

What sensation is obliteration, with a taste of eradication?

Add a dash of annihilation

Quietly glorifying hate, yet berate fate

Encase society of meretricious bobbles

Bifurcation of humanism

An altercation keeping Capitalism safe

THIS IS MINE ! ! !

As the clock ticks down to midnight

Incomprehensibilities of media indolence

Pretentious of "posting online"

The abstention of face-to-face communication

Can such distractions save a world, society or race?

Is stopping the boulder from rolling, a possibility?

Reminiscence of "living in the now"

A bygone idealism

Subterfuge of surrealism to realism

Who has the bigger nuke button?

REALLY ! ! !

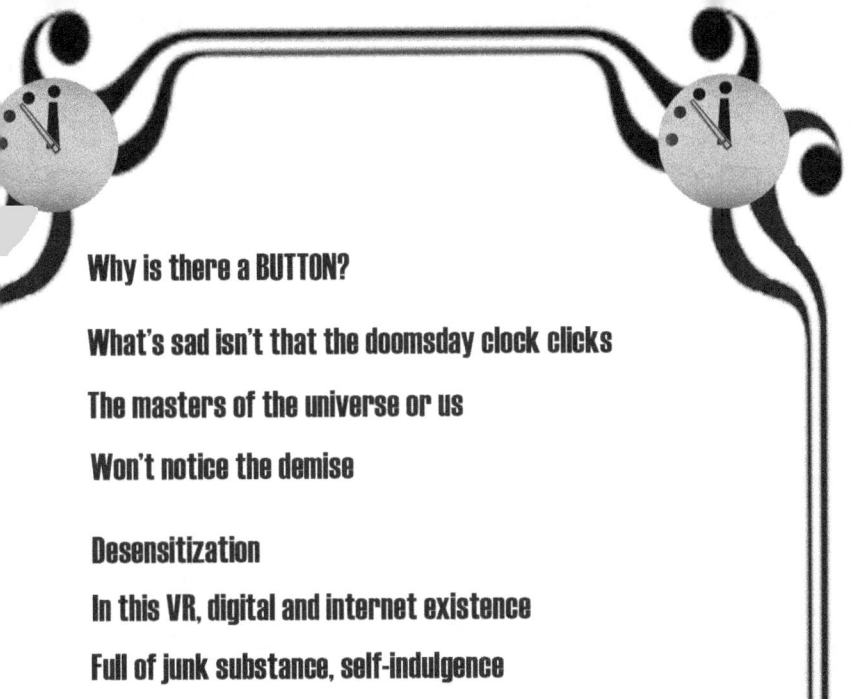

Why is there a BUTTON?

What's sad isn't that the doomsday clock clicks

The masters of the universe or us

Won't notice the demise

Desensitization

In this VR, digital and internet existence

Full of junk substance, self-indulgence

OMG! THE BACHELOR IS ON! ! !

Where's that damn remote?!?

Tick tock, tick tock, tick tock....

By Patsy Pantoja

B Boy Beats
Bella bestia brutal
Beyond Blue besos
Butchering blessed bodies.
Believing blind eyes
Balancing battles, busted botellas,
bailando, brindando, burlando,
blasting beats of
Bomba stereo.
Boom!

Alicia M. Rodriguez

MÚSICA HASTA EL FIN

A mi mami le gustaba la música
Y a mi papi le gustaba el silencio.
Cuando derrepente empezaba la cumbia,
todos bailaban mientras mi papi lloraba.

Cuando empezaba el rock, todos gritaban,
incluyendo mi papi de shock.
"Alright, ya bájenle," he would request,
while my mami would say,
"No way, súbanle!"
Y seguía el party.

Hoy, mi mami se acuerda del viejo.
Quien en las nubes, tal vez,
esta finalmente gozando su silencio
y su ajedrez.

By Claudia Mera Lam

Fabiola Manriquez

E and A

elac gives engineering and electricity
elisa, elvia, erick, elvis, and elton is eloquent
east L.A. elevates elements
elder ernie erupts and ends
exciting electrons go east
electronics and english emerge
e $=mc^2$ and elastic evolve

albert and alice are anonymous
anthony loves apples and avocados
aluminum, alloys, and algebra are awesome
aviators and alligators always appear
alcohol accounts for alliteration
avengers acknowledge articulately
alejandra allocates arrows and ammunition

A drunken captain couldn't keep
the puke in the compact compartment.
As a squad of cowards think they're fab,
Their march matches the sound of the isolated streets,
Their feet rattle, construct reasons to enter into battle.
Some trip, others rip, and another sips on liquid courage.
As the years run, as foliage ages,
pages will rage
with age.

-Christian Valles

Palabra perfumada

Poesía, piedra preciosa;
perla pura.
Pedernal pulido;
pintura perfecta.

Palabra perfumada;
pétalo púrpura.
Paisaje pintoresco;
puente plateado.

Pensamiento profético;
puerto placentero.
Paloma peregrina;
palabra perpetúa.

Raúl Macías Casas

The sky above laugh, light continues burns my sight.

The height is too much, a head rush of blood to my head.

Hush, hush, and don't talk too much.

Once hear the crunch, like a knockout punch,

You'll be done.

—Christian Valles

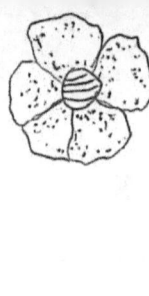

Tears

Did you hear
the veneer,
vaccum up
her tears?

Susan Chavez

Sueños.

En la noche siempre la noche donde los sueños flotan.
Despierto en la mente
mis emociones guardadas.
Durante el dia,
escondidas detras de un muro
donde no se permite desear
amar
llorar
sentir
que estas viva,
menos volar,
sigo soñando.
no despierto,
que tus emociones bailan
el baile de la libertad
banditos sueños
banditos sueños.

Ana Elizabeth Tovar

Obra majestuosa

Soy parte de la obra majestuosa de Dios.
Por mis venas corre la energía maravillosa de la vida.
Mi cuerpo es una máquina perfecta que se desplaza
sobre sus indomables pies.

Mi cabeza resguarda un cerebro de coral
impasible, incansable, inconmensurable e
impredecible, capaz de pensar, soñar y crear.

Mi ser atesora una rosa roja, radiante, reluciente
llamada corazón, protegido por un caparazón
para que no se le escape la emoción o lo engañe la razón.

Mi pensamiento es una luz inagotable que se mueve
por todos lados. A veces obscura como la amargura
o clara como la alegría.

Mis manos son pinceles que trazan la letra para
transformarla en palabras de esperanza, esfuerzo, empatía
consuelo, confianza, concordia, amor, amistad y armonía.

Raúl Macías Casas

Cooking, resting, eating
watching t.v.
doing my writing
figuring what should
I be saying

Thinking, rhyming
nothing coming out
busy looking at my
laptop.

Focusing, understanding
organizing my words
Sharing, telling, informing
So my thoughts can be
illuminating, uplifting
enriching.

MAR ☐ SOL ♥

GRACIAS A Dios

El tiempo tengo PACIENCiA y mi cuerpo encuentra la unificación!

MANTENGO PACIENCiA mientras transformo Zumos enteros de amor tradicionales

Tocando las aguas frágiles y dulces

Amor Azul

Amor azul aqui aca, atardecer
de alla, de altura sin atras.

Asi acercate acariciame y alcanza
aralla acomodando artesanos
asociados al amanecer azucarado.

Amante amado con actitud y
alimado con la aurora, mi amor de
siempre amor siempre azul.

— Judy

Una mentira

De un amor
Un amante
Un esclavo
Una cadena
Una cicatri'z
Una la'grima
Una corona
Una la'pida
Unas flores
Un traido.

Ana Elizabeth Tovar G.

In the time
of violent skies
There was a releasing
of a document
abounding in lies!

It was disheartening
to parents who were
striving to undue
all the bleeding lies,
but the parents
intrinsically knew
the Monster's cry.
Capturing their strength
releasing all fear,
the understanding parents
knew the time
was near.

Susan Chesley

A dark speck

by John Khuu

It was a speck

In the horizon

A sapling sprouted from a bad seed

An utterance without thought

A joke one night ago

Weeds and brush swayed

Darkness brewed

Storm clouds gathered, growing fatter, and the unheard grew louder

'Til a needle prick

POPulism! (but not the popular vote)

A torrent of festering hatred reigning

Consciousness aroused, contentiousness lit, conscience debated,

cautiousness abated

Umbrellas opened, fists raised, whispers howled, smoke smoldered

And when the downpour ends, there'll still be weeds and seeds

Flowers to bloom again

But a rainbow's a'comin' over the bend beyond the horizon

<<Vos, el diablotiene que salir, a supropiavoluntad, a puñaladas.
No tiene opción,la luz no quemo; nuncasana.>>
Me dice, la rana.
Mira cuando
tres titeres tristes
beben
tragos
amargos.
vos, apaga
todos
sus
recuerdos
cargados y amargados.
Vos, voy a apagar la luz,
con el trago y abrazos.
Hasta que no hay
luz.

-Christian Valles

A reaction to him:

Surreal sh x x hole
your slanderous
sorry sounds
try to scuffold us
in hate.

We sing our sounds
of sustenance,
in order to
survive your slander

Susan Chavez

Cinco Arboles

Five trees stand next to one another,
      together like a family.
Elegantly they spread their branches
      and enjoy the 360-degree view of the valley.
They become nut producers for squirrels
      and suppliers and landlords of birds.
They also become perfect hiding spots for kids
      and later for teenage lovers.
Cinco modest arboles just chilling
      and witnessing the daily circle of life.

by Claudia Mera Lam

Falling Backwards

I fell
Into a haze
I awoken inside
Another place
I've never been
It seemed familiar
But it was new.
Saw an old teacher
My piano teacher?
I never liked
He never taught
I seemed to be working at a school
He was walking behind me
Was I in his way?
He did not notice me
Or look at me
I told him,
"I was a student of yours"
But he seemed to be talking,
mumbling, responding, sort of to me
And sort of to
No one.
"Yeah, I'm a teacher,
I have students in my classroom..."
He made no sense.

I needed to get to a classroom
But I got lost
I couldn't find the right
doorway.
I kept opening
Doors.
And found
The wrong classroom
Which already had teachers!
I asked a woman who walked by
Ms. White Rabbit,
Who didn't have time for
Me or manners!
Padding to her room
SLAM
went the door!
Rude.

Then I found it!
A gymnazium of a room!
With a mountain made
Of papier-mâché...
A geology project?
So many shades of blue
Steps
Uphill steps
I must climb to get to my work door.
The teacher was behind me again
Kept making snarling sounds,
I tried move faster but
The steps were too small

Or were my feet too big?
The paper was dry and crunched
With every step as chips of paint crumbled under me
It all quickly disappeared
Then I
Appeared

in the room
I was working
Cutting paper
With scissors...
Then it happened
A person from my past
Her voice as she answered
The phone
She said her own name!
SLAM
at the receiver!
All my nerve endings
All my self esteem
GONE.
A vision of ice.
A blanket of guilt.
But for what?
I was after all working, doing all the right things, yet *fear fear fe*
Creeping all over me!
The familiar overwhelming
loss of control
Magically.
Stolen.

Her simple presence said,
'Where were you at?
They were asking about you,
I didn't know what you wanted me to tell them.
If you mess up I look bad!"

Then I looked away
My voice cracked
As I
tried to change
the subject.

by Tina Fallon

Agonía de la alegría.

Dialogaba la alegría
con su amiga ironía;
al oído le decía;
la vida es una melodía.

Contestó la ironía
que hablar de eso le aburría.
Que la vida solo era
un rato de fantasía.

No sabía la algarabía
que su prima alegría
de nostalgia se moría.

La alegría se estremecía
en su lecho de agonía;
a todos entristecía
ésta fatal pesadilla.

Si moría la alegría
ya no habría algarabía
y a todos dejaría
sufriendo su propia agonía.

Raúl Macías Casas

It feels like I'm...

Being punished for an attempted jail break to get out this

mass produced

hole for the soulless,

brought you by

faceless sponsor,

who knows your

underwear,

and

you're

shoe size

As if my past life was of a mole,

a blind existence,

scratching new path in unfamiliar territories.

If they see the sunlight, their blinded for life;

if one cries out of frustration,

It begs to be heard,

only to be left behind,

by his own herd

a new strange sensation,

salvation while swinging on a rope.

—Christian Valls.

Rebuilding Me
By Rocio Diaz

Strong I became
Que yo solita lo tuve que hacer
Rebuild, me
But first I had to get rid of the guilt; that spilt
In order to rebuild
So I began to reknit, my soul like a quilt
So it would no longer tilt

Porque el dolor fue tan grande
Que yo ya no necesito que ande,
para que me mande

Primordial

Al final que me voy a llevar?
lo primordial, de mi madre el
resital, de mi hija lo jovial, de
mis hermanos lo inusual, de mi
mundo lo ambiental y de los demas
lo angelical.

—Judy

Removing Fetters

All arises and passes away
nothing stays the same way,
with this you don't play
there's no way to stay.

It's all about Karma
on the path of Dharma.
Cause and effect invoked,
what I do matters
my life is in tatters.

One day, I caught a glance
this thing called impermanence,
so I made it my stance.
Watching pleasure and pain
there's a balance to gain.

Once provoked
now unmoving,
tolerance
takes proving.

No me, no my
I ask myself why?

Breathing my breath
is all I have left,
everything is lighter
my grip no longer tighter.

Selflessness a love
that rises above,
a perfection, a parami
extended to all that be.

in silence, insights unveil
ultimate truth without fail.
This walk I have chosen
wisdom interwoven.

Respiro para adentro
respiro para afuera,
es lo que me queda.

Con todo el esfuerzo
propósito de mi estancia,
sobrepaso obstáculos
como la de mi importancia.

Por ultimo renuncio
todos los gustos de mi existencia,
nunca lograron darme
ni un paso con cadencia.

Te ofrezco este regalo
y todo lo que tengo,
me agrada el desapego,
por eso lo reparto
ya no quiero ataduras
de eso estoy harto.

Luz Donis

the chase   karyn g.

innocent inchoate idea
i am chasing you
breathless, empty, exhausted.

unbelievably beyond absurd absolutions
reaching to reclaim my right
to hold you

yet you flitter out of touch, transcend
the bounds of cognition
fly to the furthest safe place

and i am lost.

why did I not write it down???

Night as the new trend, I dreamt of a dripping death,
as it drains my brain in a dreadful bed.
As I fed Zed, the pet, it said,
"She loves in shells of seas in tears,
runs in years of fears."
In my confusion, I said,
"Did Sassy Sam snap a photo of me?"
Quickly, I snapped back.
"Hack," he said only to clap back,
"The treasonous traitor, a troublemaker he is."

-Christian Valles

Mi Cielo, Te Quiero, Te Tengo

Baldwin Hills Library–Group Poem

Mi cielo, te quiero, te tengo.
Kiss as sweet as a mango,
dance conmigo fandango.
Corazón relampago,

you illuminate my soul
como un caliente sol.

The Cat Sat on the Mat

Junipero Serra Library–Group Poem

The cat sat on the mat as
the Spanish man spat, "Who
dat in the hat, eating that kit-kat."

Meow was how the cow had to
bow to hear the sound, however,
Issac, excited, surprised his nine
wives with a diamond mine.

The feline made a beeline towards
the treeline, street signs, and got
deep fried. So much for nine lives.

On My Way to Growing Up, I

Ben Franklin Library—Group Poem

On my way to growing up, I,
then found myself asking you why
for all the times you said goodbye.

Eres mi mejor tequila
y mi mejor harmonía
y mi peor pesadilla.

In my life, one way is to fight,
with you, my wife, I found my light.

About the Conchas y Café program

Conchas y Café is a 10-week workshop series for adults, focusing exclusively on creative writing, literacy, and illustration. Participants have the opportunity to work with volunteer writers and artists on developing artwork that will be published and presented in a quarterly 'zine and public reading.

For more information, locations, and dates for upcoming Conchas y Café workshops, contact us by email at *info@DSTLArts.org* today.

Acerca el programa Conchas y Café

Conchas y Café es un taller de 10 semanas para adultos, especializando en escritura, literatura, y dibujo. Participantes tienen la oportunidad de trabajar con escritores y artistas voluntarios en el desarrollo de obras de arte que serán publicados y presentados en publicaciones trimestrales y lecturas públicas.

Para más información, localidades, y fechas de próximos talleres de Conchas y Café, contáctenos por correo electronico al *info@DSTLArts.org*.

This program is supported in part by:

Zapata-King Neighborhood Council

West Adams Neighborhood Council

About the Authors
Sobre los autores

John Khuu

John first wrote his name at age six, but began writing poetry at sixteen. These days he opts for the meticulously crafted haiku to snapshot a moment's essence. Longer form poems provide glimpses into a flurry of his thoughts and enable him to ponder the heart of the matter.

David Mangas

Escritor, poeta. Naufragó en la isla "Conchas y Café" desde dónde nos manda su canto que resbala en la conciencia y moja al espíritu. Viejo pirata de los mares Californianos.

Nikolai Garcia

Nikolai Garcia grew up in South Central; currently lives in Compton; and works in East Hollywood. With the help of DSTL Arts, he is currently working on a manuscript for a poetry chapbook

Patsy Pantoja

A blossoming writer, Patsy enjoys being with the writing group. Our weekly prompts is her way of inspiration.

Oscar Palencia

My name is Oscar Palencia and I am excited to share my stories and continue to be empowered to write. I am a Raiders fan and love traveling to different cities for sports games. I enjoy watching movies and attending the annual horrorthon in Santa Monica. I am an avid graphic novel reader and am currently reading the Avengers.

Suzanne Im

Suzanne is a lifelong book lover who currently works as a librarian in Los Angeles. While her professional life has revolved around collecting, organizing, and providing access to the work of others, she has always wanted to write and publish a book of her own. A daughter of Cambodian immigrants, her work delves into issues of identity, class struggle, and the lingering aftermath of trauma.

Nancy Yvette Hernandez

Nancy Yvette Hernandez was born on June 11, 1984 in Los Angeles, California. She was raised in her grandparents' house in South Los Angeles, where she got most of her inspiration. Her passion for writing didn't come till her late 20's.

Cinthia "mar-I-sol" Lozano

Cinthia "mar-I-sol" Lozano is an artist and writer living in L.A., and spreading the value of the arts through her personal arts and teaching artist practice. Her contributions to the Conchas y Café Zine are much appreciated.

Abraham Jaramillo

Abraham Jaramillo is a multimedia artist; illustrator, graphic designer, and photographer. His love for the arts began back when he created small sketch galleries for his grandmother when he was 8 years old. A longtime volunteer and teaching artist with DSTL Arts, Abraham enjoys and nurtures the pursuit of knowledge both in himself and others.

Karyn Grasse

Karyn is a Monterey Park native and has been writing short stories and poems since she was 12. Sometimes, they get published. Sometimes, they sit in a box. Her most treasured creative endeavor, however, is the charming little person who has invaded her life for the past three years.

Rocio Diaz

Rocio Diaz is a first generation undocumented woman recently graduated from Cal State Los Angeles. She's a Mexicana poet, playwright, dancer, advocate, and artivist. Rocio made her debut as a writer at Casa 0101 with her writings *Pink Scars*, *Tired*, and her most recent, *Once Upon A Time… Con DACA*. She wants to thank her family for being her unconditional love, support, and rock. "Familia, los amo!"

Judith Larson

Mi nombre es Judith A. Larson. Nací en la Ciudad de México, pero crecí en el Valle Sagrado de Tepoztlán, Morelos. Soy una mujer apasionada de la vida, de mi familia y de mi hija, quien está en la foto. Amante del arte en toda su expresión, estoy empezando a descubrir que sí, todos tenemos algo de locos y poetas.

Raúl Macias Casas

Raúl Macias Casas nació el 9 de enero de 1960 en Saucillo, Chihuahua, se crió en la Ciudad de México. Su inquietud por escribir surge durante su adolescencia como una forma de explicarse la esencia de la vida. Forma parte del taller literario Conchas y Café desde el año 2016. Sus trabajos de poesía han aparecido en varios libros colectivos publicados por DSTL Arts.

Eddie Hall White, Jr.

Eddie Hall White, Jr. is a former teacher, poet, playwright, screenwriter, and novelist. His plays include *Adventures in Paradise*, *Will There Ever Be a Morning*, and *Misadventures in Paradise*. His screenplays include, *Learning to Love Myself*, and *It Was Always You*. Eddie Hall White, Jr.'s novel, *Oh, Baby, Oh* will be published soon.

Ana C. Holton

Ana C. Holton, guatemalteca, maestra de profesión, escritora, cocinera y jardinera, por pasión. Dueña del café literario "Vagón del Tiempo" en Guatemala. Ha participado en muchos talleres literarios, con Marco Antonio Flores, Raúl de La Horra, Elias Barahona, entre otros. Escribe poesía y cuento.

Mauricio Moreno

Mauricio is a writer hailing from New Jersey who's mission is to help make the world a more interconnected one by writing stories and sharing the experiences of people who feel they don't have a voice. A lover of all forms of art and written word, Mauricio has written several poems, short stories, and haikus, and is working on a novel and screenplay. Most recently, he is working on a collection of poetry to be released in 2018.

Michelle Smith

Michelle Smith is a poet and artist working toward producing work that emits love and empathy for people of all kinds. She is a welcome addition to our Conchas y Café Zine family of artists.

Fabiola Manríquez

Having the blessing to partake in Conchas y Café has strengthened my confidence as a writer and artist. It has given me the freedom to release incredible personal stories with character and grace. My aspiration is to help others discover parallel endeavors.

Alicia M. Rodriguez

Alicia proudly represents her heritage and family through her writing, and as the Outreach Librarian for the Los Angeles Public Library, she happily helps her community gain access to valuable resources the libraries provide.

David Fallon

In the early 2000s, David Fallon published a handful of plays, poems, and stories. He took a 10 year sabbatical to build a career and raise a son. The recent death of his mother prompted him to return to writing– primarily short stories and an upcoming novel.

Ziba Zehdar-Gazdecki

Ziba is the co-author of the Zebra Pizza Zine, amd currently the Young Adult Librarian at the Baldwin Hills Branch Library, home of the first Los Angeles Public Library Zine Library. An avid zinester, DJ, and more, Ziba's creativity knows no bounds.

Ana Elizabeth Tovar

Ana Elizabeth Tovar-Gonzales is a lifetime student of the arts, who grew up in La Joya, Puanas, Durango, Mexico. Her work explores elements of realism taken from personal experiences to create rich narratives.

Tina Fallon

Tina Fallon has a Bachelor of the Arts from Cal Poly Pomona. She started writing in high school, stopped, began again in the early 90s, stopped, then started again in 2016! She lives with her husband and son in South Pasadena.

Susan Chavez

Grandmother to two, mother of three, an artist, an educator, a writer who's passion is fueled by social justice. I'm so grateful to the East L.A. Tuesday evening writing group for the depth and breadth of their unending support.

Christian Valles

Christian Valles is a visual artist and educator who grew up in the city of Bell, CA. His work often features elements of realism juxtaposed with the potential for escape and transcendence that exists in all urban spaces. Christian also publishes a biannual zine, "Mi Desorden" in which he showcases his commitment to capturing urban landscapes.

Claudia Mera Lam

Claudia Mera Lam is a LA-based writer originally from Mexico City. She is currently working on her first memoir and other fun projects. She is consistently curious and is always up for new adventures– whether it's across the 405 or on the other side of the world.

Luz Donis

Second generation Guatemalan, raised in Boyle Heights. Trained and worked as a nurse for L.A. County and L.A. Unified. Currently immersed in Vipassana meditation and Buddhist studies.

This publication was produced by DSTL Arts.

DSTL Arts is a nonprofit arts mentorship organization that inspires, teaches, and hires emerging artists from underserved communities.

To learn more about DSTL Arts, visit online at:

DSTLArts.org

 @DSTLArts

 /DSTLArts